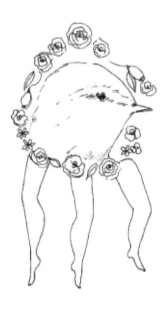

Luna Miguel has given us a world of birds with purposes. Birds to eat, birds that ejaculate on prostitutes, birds that mock and birds that mourn. Birds that live in monotonous places and birds made of ink. The birds of Luna's poetry do something or see something or are something and like the poet herself give us a brilliant insight to an otherwise sorry world.

Kendra Grant Malone

Luna is great. There are no poems like hers. She carries herself through them like some ageless spirit of unchecked wisdom, but she doesn't tell you what she knows. If I read this book six thousand years from now in a different body on a different planet, I still wouldn't know what Luna knows. How is she so damn smart?

Matthew Savoca

Like other sublime things, Luna Miguel's Bluebird and Other Tattoos acts in several emotional hemispheres at once: tongues, brains, bloods, a darker comfort, a good pale wood, fields of nettles, fingertips, several sorts of well-kept flesh, pulsation, relief. "I have seen my generation renounce literature," she writes. "I have seen it and I am not interested." Assured yet compassionate, stark yet starving, what comes through in these poems is a great sense of heat like intense sun, and focused as a score of skin-rendered lines born under pressure, calm like why "The neon always hits my shirt / and crosses the crystals / of the transport in which I habit... I hear the dizziness of who does not travel... Here panic does not exist."

Blake Butler

Luna Miguel is a poet who can make me cry. Her passion for life and for poetry is uncommon. She makes language concise, supple, and exciting again. Recurring images: of birds, disease, spit, and blood, integral to a mortal, embodied poetry that reminds us 'Death cannot be experienced neither for the living nor the dead but for the sick.' Luna writes a poem, 'The Beautiful World Gives Me Disgust.' She writes, 'I exist, therefore, / then I tremble.' She writes of the suicidal poets, she writes of all women, she writes of the young. She writes knowing it's a lie, she lives in the shadow of death. Luna writes of her 'unprotected life,' her 'unprotected diary.' There is no comfort in this poetry, there is hard beauty. 'The wind was this. Being born was this. Dying without dying and without a disease was this. To tell you the truth: I am here and I need you.' Luna.

Stephen Tully Dierks

Some planets have rings around them. Luna has words. While reading her book, I imagined birds rotating around her and herself spinning around each word.

Ana Carrete

Bluebird and Other Tattoos

Bluebird y Otros Tatuajes

selected poems

Luna Miguel

Translated by Jeremy Spencer

Scrambler Books 2012
Sacramento, California

Bluebird and Other Tattoos/Bluebird y Otros Tatuajes
©2012 Luna Miguel
English translations ©2012 by Jeremy Spencer

Published by Scrambler Books
Sacramento, California
www.scramblerbooks.com
Translation series no.1

This is the first time Luna Miguel's poems have been published in English in the United States. All poems were originally written in Spanish by Luna Miguel.

Cover art and design as well as all drawings inside by Betty Blue

1st Paperback edition
ISBN: 978-0-578-09890-6
Printed in the USA

Bluebird and Other Tattoos is a selection of poems from the various works of Luna Miguel: *Estar enfermo* (La Bella Varsovia), *Poetry is not dead* (DVD Ediciones), *Pensamientos estériles* (El Cangrejo Pistolero Ediciones) and *Sailor's Grave* (the next publication). All of those collections were published first in Spain.

Introduction

A bird is an animal like no other. It has a beak, wings, feathers. Most are social creatures that tend to migrate. And. They sing. A bird's song can be beautiful. It can be violent. It can be a warning. A bird can sing for many reasons, the most important of which, to communicate.

The poems you are about to read are in their own way versions of calls, cries, chants, and warbles. They are unbreakable. They are the poetry of youth. They are already broken. They are the prose of development. They are ferocious. They are graceful.

Luna Miguel born and raised in Spain is considered a Spanish writer. Luna Miguel born and raised in Spain should be considered much more than a Spanish writer. She writes so that anyone can understand her words. She writes searching for the reality within a feeling, the reality within a situation. Her words can be soft. Her words can be harsh. Her poems are music.

*

Translating is a difficult thing. At least for me. There is a constant struggle between the *meaning* of the words, and of the phrases in the original language as compared to how a translator chooses to represent them in the translated language. With these English translations of Luna's poems, I am attempting to keep the actual words that Luna writes with, without losing the sentiments, without losing the meaning that Luna conveys in her poems. I hope I have been successful. Any inadequacies in the translations are all on me.

I must thank Aaron Dailey for his constant willingness to help with and confer about random words and phrases in Spanish and English. I owe the deepest gratitude to Concepcion "Concha" Romero Jimenez because without her assistance, these translations would not be nearly as clear and sharp. Repeatedly, she was always enthusiastic to discuss, edit and suggest better translations for this book. Thank you Concha. Thank you as well to Ana Carrete for her help and willingness to read and edit this manuscript and for her words. Also thank you to Kendra Grant Malone, Matthew Savoca, Richard Chiem, Stephen Tully Dierks, Blake Butler, Antonio J. Rodríguez and everyone that has supported Luna and Scrambler Books. E tambem muito obrigado ao meu amor Cyntia.

Over the last 2 years, I have had the immense pleasure of getting to know Luna. She is a friend and I am honored that she has allowed me the enjoyment of undertaking this project and letting Scrambler Books publish *Bluebird and Other Tattoos*. I appreciate her kindness, her patience, her friendship, her support and her help with this book and with all things related to Scrambler Books. I adore her writing, as does all of Spain and Europe, and hopefully now with this edition she will receive the proper introduction that she deserves in the United States. I could not ask for a better writer or a better person to be associated with.

Jeremy Spencer
December 2012
Woodland, California

There's a bluebird in my heart
that wants to get out.
CHARLES BUKOWSKI

passer mortuus est meae puellae
passer, deliciae meae puellae
quem plus illa oculis suis amabat
CATULO

Señor
La jaula se ha vuelto pájaro
Qué haré con el miedo
ALEJANDRA PIZARNIK

Un pájaro de papel en el pecho
dice que el tiempo de los besos no ha llegado;
vivir, vivir, el sol cruje invisible,
besos o pájaros, tarde o pronto o nunca.
VICENTE ALEIXANDRE

sick rose
(2005-2008)

sick rose

(2005-2008)

SÍNTOMAS

I

garganta vacía, blando, duro, cabeza.
garganta seca, fiebre, sueño, tripa.
tengo todos los síntomas, sueño todas
las enfermedades. sangre, frío, azúcar.

no estoy enamorada.

SYMPTOMS

I
empty throat, soft, hard, head.
dry throat, fever, sleepy, gut.
i have all the symptoms, dream of all
the sicknesses. blood, cold, sugar.

i am not in love.

II
sin que nada doliera

los dioses

decidieron cortarnos
la garganta

II
with nothing hurt

the gods

decided to cut
our throat

III

pronuncias la epidemia
y un hombre muere

pronuncias el silencio
que nos queda

III
pronounce the epidemic
and a man dies

pronounce the silence
that we remain

IV
de la poesía espero maldad

exijo asco

invoco enfermedad

IV
from poetry i hope evil

i demand disgust

i invoke disease

V
no son poemas

lo que lees son mentiras

V
they are not poems

what you read are lies

MUSA ENFERMA

Musa torpe: las paredes te observan
con mirada de gato
moribundo.

Has escrito todo cuanto debías escribir,
cantado cuanto podías ocultar,
pronunciado con vergüenza el nombre del desierto

¿ y ahora qué te queda?

Musa de música humillante.
Pájaro del monótono árbol.
Enemiga de tu propio verso.

SICK MUSE

Clumsy muse: the walls observe you
with the gaze of a dying
cat.

You have written everything that you had to write,
sung all that was hidden,
pronounced with embarrassment the deserted name

and now what do you have left?

Muse of humiliating music.
Bird of the monotonous tree.
An enemy of your own verse.

QUINCE AÑOS

Detesté al nacer.

Odié durante toda mi infancia.

A la edad de quince años,
empecé a hacer el amor.

FIFTEEN YEARS

I detested since birth.

I hated throughout my childhood.

At the age of fifteen,
I began to make love.

POEMA Y CIGARRO

Cien horas bajo el cri-cri de las margaritas.
Dedos cruzados para que vuelvas pronto.
Cortinas cerradas hasta que el sol me reclame.

Cien horas donde Venus no daña.

Coge las tijeras y aparta la mirada.

POEM AND CIGARETTE

One hundred hours under the cricket call of daisies.
Fingers crossed for a quick return.
Curtains closed until the sun reclaims me.

One hundred hours where Venus does no damage.

Take the scissors and look away.

SUEÑO

Soñé que atrapaba
gorriones al vuelo.

Apretaba
sus barrigas redonditas
con el dedo índice.

Arañaba
sus patas grises
para limpiar la arena.

Devoraba al pájaro
en su último canto.

En su último intento
de volar,

acarició mi estómago.

DREAM

I dreamt that I caught
flying sparrows.

Pressed
their little round bellies
with my index finger.

Scratched
their gray legs
to clean off the sand.

I devoured the bird
on its last song.

On its last attempt
to fly,

it caressed my stomach.

SICK ROSE

No.
No vas de luto estricto.

Aún sangra rojo tu corazón.

SICK ROSE

No.
You are not in strict mourning.

Your heart still bleeds red.

TENTATIVA DE CELOS

¿Cómo se vive en un abismo sin profundidad, amor mío?
MARINA TSVIETÁIEVA

Las otras mujeres se ríen de mí
porque soy hermosa
hasta con los labios rotos.

Porque no tengo
pestañas,
porque no llevo
medias.

Porque la ropa me estorba junto al poema
y el poema me viste cuando lloro.

Las otras y los demás no saben nada.

No leen cuanto escupo.

No olfatean cuanto expulso.

Los otros y el mundo ríen
porque soy hermosa.

ATTEMPT AT JEALOUSY

How do you live in an abyss without depth, my love?
MARINA TSVIETÁIEVA

The other women laugh at me
because I am beautiful
even with broken lips.

Because I do not have
eyelashes,
because I do not wear
tights.

Because my clothes hinder me next to the poem
and the poems dress me when I cry.

The others and the rest of the women know nothing.

They do not read all that I spit.

They do not smell all that I expel.

The others and the world laugh
because I am beautiful.

VOGLIO PARTIRE DI QUESTO PIANETA

No oigo. Qué ves.
Siempre es lo mismo cuando vuelvo,
cuando él,
cuando alguien,
cuando me espera y no hay nada.

Siempre la humedad de la pared.
Sin agua.
Sin ascensor.
Sin mantequilla.

La ciudad parece animada.
No conseguimos escuchar mis pensamientos.

Sé que no quiero quedarme en este planeta.

I WANT TO LEAVE FROM THIS PLANET

I do not hear. What you see.
It is always the same when I return,
when he,
when someone,
when someone waits and there is nothing.

Always moisture from the wall.
Without water.
Without lift.
Without butter.

The city seems lively.
We could not hear my thoughts.

I know that I do not want to stay on this planet.

el neón de siempre
(2008-2009)

good old neon
(2008-2009)

CAVE LUNAM

Cuidado.

Mi gripe es porcina y maligna.
Mi gripe es de Vaca y de Ave loca.
Mi gripe es Nietzsche tan mal traducido.

Presta atención a mis venas hinchadas,
dentro guardo las babas de Panero.
Dentro, el corazón de un Huevo Kinder
sin sorpresa:
Sylvia Plath Muerta,
David Foster Wallace Muerto,
Virginia, estilo mariposa, Muerta.

Atención. Bandera púrpura.
La gripe de las almas.
La gripe del humo.
La gripe de las codas y la tipografía
desplumada.

Atención. Contagian.

Cuidado.

Muerdo.

CAVE LUNAM

Be careful.

My flu is swine and malignant.
My flu is mad cow and bird.
My flu is badly translated Nietzsche.

Pay attention to my swollen veins,
I keep Panero's drool inside them.
Inside, the heart of a Kinder Egg
without a surprise:
Sylvia Plath Deceased,
David Foster Wallace Deceased,
Virginia, butterfly style, Deceased.

Attention. Purple flag.
The flu of souls.
The flu of smoke.
The flu of the codas and the plucked
typography

Attention. They are contagious.

Be careful.

I bite.

LADRAS O MUERES

También he visto a los mejores cerebros de mi generación

destruidos por el emoticono.

He visto sus rostros inexpresivos.

He leído sus poemas fotocopiados.

No conozco su violencia

pero intuyo un nuevo aullido.

Un grito seco.

Un grito de amor.

Porque también he amado a los mejores cerebros de mi
generación:

los he besado y masticado,

los he deseado tanto.

Cerebros que vienen del cielo

cegados por una luz que no parecía suficiente

y que ahora quema la entraña

de mis antiguos versos.

Cerebros que he sido y cerebros que seré.

BARK OR DIE

I have also seen the best minds of my generation

destroyed by the emoticon.

I have seen their inexpressive faces.

I have read their photocopied poems.

I do not know their violence

but I sense a new howl.

A dry scream.

A scream of love.

Because I have also loved the best minds of my generation:

I have kissed and chewed them,

I have desired them so much.

Minds that come from the sky

blinded by a light that was not sufficient

and now burns the entrails

of my old verses.

Minds that I have been and minds that I will be.

Drogas que he consumido. Medicinas.

Bocas que he rechazado y que ahora necesito.

Sesos de animal que mi madre cocinaba

antes de cambiar de ciudad

y dejar

las cucarachas del armario

en el olvido.

Cerebros recitando de memoria.

Cerebros escribiendo de memoria.

Ignorantes neuronas

vomitando de memoria.

He visto la generación a la que pertenezco y apenas la soporto.

He visto a mi generación renegar de la literatura.

La he visto y no me interesa.

La he visto y me parezco demasiado.

La he visto muerta.

Drugs that I have consumed. Medicines.

Mouths that I have rejected and now need.

Animal brains that my mother would cook

before changing cities

and to leave

the cockroaches of the cupboard

in oblivion.

Minds reciting from memory.

Minds writing from memory.

Ignorant neurons

vomiting memory.

I have seen the generation to which I belong and I hardly support it.

I have seen my generation renounce literature.

I have seen it and I am not interested.

I have seen it and I look too much.

I have seen it dead.

PARQUE DE LOS YONKIS

¿quién cojones se libra de su parte repugnante?
ANGÉLICA LIDDELL

En el parque de mi ventana
hay flores de un solo color.

Blanquecinas como papilla,
huelen a fruta madura.

Miro el paisaje pequeño.
Sentada, junto al tocadiscos
y Daft Punk.

Apoyada sobre el cristal,
flores breves
entran por las rendijas.

Miro.
En el parque hay chustas
y jeringas.

Blanquecinas como las venas,

mis heridas
huelen a néctar.

PARK OF THE JUNKIES

Who the hell can escape from the repugnant part?
ANGÉLICA LIDDELL

In the park from my window
there are flowers of only one color.

Whitish like baby food,
they smell of ripe fruit.

I look at the small landscape.
Sitting, next to the turntable
and Daft Punk.

Resting on the glass,
short flowers
fit in the cracks.

I look.
In the park there are roaches
and syringes.

Whitish like veins

my wounds
smell of nectar.

RED BULL SIN AZÚCAR

*Traté de deslizar la mano por debajo
de la suya, pero me la apartó.
— No, es más rápido sola.*
J. G. BALLARD

Ahora,
ver porno.

Porque es junio y hace calor
en mi alma.
Porque
qué
mejor sino ver
porno.

¿Escribir?
¿Leer poemas de amor?

Qué mejor
que el placer
de una felación
de alguien
que no soy yo
a otro alguien
que no soy yo
para confirmar
mi existencia.

Me masturbo mal.
Finjo un orgasmo.
Me deshidrato.
Escribo para quienes conocen
mi mentira.

RED BULL WITHOUT SUGAR

I tried to slide the hand below hers,
but she pushed it away.
— No, it's faster alone.
J.G. BALLARD

Now,
watch porn.

Because it's june and very hot
in my soul.
Because
what
better than to watch
porn?

To write?
To read love poems?

What better
than the pleasure
of a fellatio
from someone
that is not me to
another someone
that is not me
to confirm
my existence.

I masturbate wrong.
Pretend an orgasm.
I dehydrate.
I write for those who know
my lie.

Porque miento en esta tecla,
porque engendro
máscaras con la lengua,
porque veo el filme
y lloro la caricia,

porque no sé decir no
a Otro maldito yo.

Because I'm lying in this keystroke,
because I conceive
masks with the tongue,
because I watch the film
and weep for the caress,

because I cannot say no
to Another damned me.

POESÍA ORTODOXA

Ortodoxa
sin haber comulgado.

Cristiana
sin bautizo.

Santa
por dibujar estigmas
con el flujo
de mi sexo.

ORTHODOX POETRY

Orthodox
without having received communion.

Christian
without baptism.

Saintly
by drawing stigmas
with the fluids
of my sex.

JUVENTUD

Pequeña prostituta,

pájaros carnívoros
eyaculan sobre tus alas

y sin embargo vuelas.

YOUTH

Little prostitute,

carnivorous birds
ejaculate on your wings

and nevertheless you fly.

GARGANTA DEL HOMBRE SONORO

Este beso no es de nadie:

pertenece al mundo que no soportamos,
al mundo que pesa en los brazos mitológicos,
al mundo asco y mundo nieve que rueda,
despacio,
por el hueco de las arterias.

Mi libertad comienza
donde comienza este beso.

Los minutos secos
carecen de importancia,
la saliva
es tuya
la saliva
es mía
la saliva es el cielo
si la expulso y cae
sobre tus pies.

Dedos negros, no limpio
lo que no me pertenece,
ni tu voz,
ni tu suciedad,
ni tu sangre fuerte.

Dedos negros, pájaros.

Pájaros suicidas resuenan
en mí como el miedo
en tu garganta alta.

THROAT OF THE SONOROUS MAN

This kiss is not anyone's:

it belongs to the world that we do not support,
the heavy world in the mythological arms,
the disgusting world and snow world that rolls
slowly,
for the hollow of the arteries.

My freedom begins
where this kiss begins.

The dry minutes
are not important,
saliva
is yours
saliva
is mine
saliva is the sky
expelled and fallen
on your feet.

Black fingers, I don't clean
what is not mine,
nor your voice
nor your suicide
nor your lucky blood.

Black fingers, birds.

Suicidal birds resonate
in me as fear
in your high throat.

Pájaros que incordian.

Pájaros que mienten
sobre cada beso.

Birds that annoy.

Birds that lie
about each kiss.

DE CAMINO A LA VÍA LÁCTEA

Tan sólo discreción es mi reclamo.

Tan sólo discreción, poeta,
que esos versos no son tuyos.

Tan sólo excreción celeste.
Introspección violácea.
Color sin adjetivo
y alas de rosa enferma.

No quiero saber de economía.
No quiero saber la Crisis.
No me interesan mis hijos,
ni el terrorismo,
ni tampoco su voz.

Qué le vamos a pedir al poema sino una piedra de coca.

Qué le voy a pedir al espejo sino una hilera de hormigas
penetrando en mi trasero.

Qué le voy a pedir al poeta
si cada vez que lo invoco se olvida de mí.

Hormiga.
Poeta.

Tan sólo tu silencio es mi reclamo.

ROAD TO THE MILKY WAY

Discretion is my only claim.

Only discretion, poet,
that these verses are not yours.

Only celestial excretion.
Violet introspection.
Color without adjective
and wings of a sick rose.

I don't want to know the economy.
I don't want to know the Crisis.
I am not interested in my children,
nor terrorism,
nor his voice.

What can we ask of the poem but a rock of cocaine.

What will I ask of the mirror but a line of ants
penetrating my ass.

What will I ask of the poet
if every time I invoke him he forgets about me.

Ant.
Poet.

Your silence is my only claim.

NOTTURNO 223

El neón de siempre azota mi camisa
y traspasa los cristales
del transporte en el que habito.

Autobuses circulares,
ruedas blandas,
búhos.

Giran como giró el miedo en mi estómago
el día seis de mayo de 2009,
a las ocho cero cero horas,
durante el accidente.

Siluetas,
campos de óxido,
prostitutas negras.

Olvido el kilómetro presente.
Escucho el mareo de quien no viaja.

Aquí no existe el pánico:

ticket
asiento áspero
olor.

Reconozco mi reflejo en los cristales,
le pregunto qué poema escribiré esta noche
qué tragedia escribiré esta noche
con qué temor escribiré esta noche.

NOCTURNE 223

The neon always hits my shirt
and crosses the crystals
of the transport in which I habit.

Circular buses,
soft wheels,
owls.

Spin and turn like the fear in my stomach
the day may sixth 2009
at eight hundred hours,
during the accident.

Silhouettes,
oxide fields,
black prostitutes.

I forget the present kilometer.
I hear the dizziness of who does not travel.

Here panic does not exist:

ticket
rough seat
odor.

I recognize my reflection in the crystals,
I ask him the poem to write at night
the tragedy to write tonight
with what fear to write tonight.

Prostitutas del polígono.
Retrato Nuevas Musas y ellas me regalan
el último verso:

autobús nocturno,
dársena 10.

Tiempo recuperado en los transportes públicos.

Polygon prostitutes.
New Muses portrayal and they give me
the last verse:

nocturnal bus,
dock 10.

Recovered time on public transport.

NOTTURNO 223 (II)

de noche,
salían a la calle en Madrid como quien sale
al mundo
OLVIDO GARCÍA VALDÉS

Es tarde,
alguien vomita en el asiento de al lado.

Un hilo
oscuro
recorre el vehículo
hasta el último asiento,

y huele a sexo.

Es de noche
Madriz se extiende con la luz.

(Me obsesionan los polígonos,
las prostitutas vacías, y siento
que ya he hablado antes de esto).

Avenida de América:
salgo de la Villa
como quien abandona el mundo.

Un olor
oscuro
recorre el vehículo.

A mi lado alguien,
ebrio de dolor,
vomita

NOCTURNE 223 (II)

at night,
took to the street in Madrid as one leaves
the world
OLVIDO GARCÍA VALDÉS

It's late,
someone vomits in the passenger seat.

A yarn
dark
runs through the vehicle
to the last seat,

and smells like sex.

It's night time
Madriz extends with the light.

(I'm obsessed with the polygons,
empty prostitutes, and I feel
I have already talked about this before).

Avenue of America:
I leave the Villa
as one who abandons the world.

An odor
dark
runs through the vehicle.

On my side someone,
drunk from pain,
vomits

lo breve
de mi noche.

briefly
from my night.

NOTTURNO 223 (III)

Acabaré escribiendo
cualquier cosa
menos poesía.

Acabaré ahogada
en la sábana,
en la cama verde
que no alcanzo
cama
a la que no llego
por este camino
ruidoso.

Autobús: casa.

Argelinos dormidos.
Maricas que respiran
rápido
como si vivieran al borde
de la muerte.

Transporte atestado: casa.

Acabaré mareada
en la cuneta
dos euros ochenta y cinco
céntimos.

Y a cada hora el trayecto
es más
peligroso.
Y a cada hora
la cama

NOCTURNE 223 (III)

I will end up writing
anything
but poetry.

I will end up
in the sheet
in the green bed
that I can't reach
bed
that I can't get
through this
noisy road.

Bus: home.

Algerians asleep.
Queers that breath
fast
as if living on the edge
of death.

Crowded transportation: home.

I will end up dizzy
in the ditch
two euros eighty five
cents.

And every hour the journey
is more
dangerous
and every hour
the bed

es más
extraña.

Acabaré mandando
Continental Auto
a la mierda.

Porque la vida
es cualquier cosa
menos poesía.

Porque qué tiene
de poético
el miedo hoy
en mi carne.

Acabaré haciendo
cualquier otra cosa
menos
poesía.

Porque no es lo que tú.

Ni lo que yo.

Porque no es lo que el mundo
necesita.

is more
strange.

I will end up sending
Continental Auto
to hell.

Because life
is anything
but poetry.

Because what does it have
from poetic
fear today
in my flesh.

I will end up doing
any other thing
but
poetry.

Because that is not what you.

Nor what I.

Because that is not what the world
needs.

DÁRSENA 10: POETIQUE DE LA VILLE

De las horas que he esperado aquí o allá, el minuto de las gaviotas parece único. ¿De qué pájaro se trata? ¿Por qué lo envidio? ¿Puedo aplicar el término manada, el término orquesta, el término cielo, *ejército aviar*, aquí, mientras espero? ¿Hay gaviotas en Madriz? ¿Hay mar? ¿Por qué las veo? Y no me refiero al pájaro franquista, ni al pollo asado del *take away*, ni al símbolo conservador. Eso no me interesa aquí ni allá. De eso no hablo aquí ni allá. Las nubes son una bandada de estrellas naranjas. Aquí y ahora eres tú el protagonista. Querido gorrión. Mi amada ha muerto. Pero no tergiverses las palabras de Catulo. No tatúes las cenizas en tu boca. Querido gorrión, ¿bajo qué forma naciste? Y no me refiero al poema, no me refiero a la filosofía ni al arte; sí al espacio y al humo de todas las horas en las que espero, en las que leo, en las que Madriz es un desierto. De todas las horas en las que huyo. En las que no te tengo.

DOCK 10: POETRY OF THE CITY

Of the hours that I have waited here or there, the minute of the gulls seems unique. Which bird is it? Why do I envy it? Can I apply the term flock, the term orchestra, the term sky, *avian army*, here, while I wait? Are there gulls in Madriz? Is there a sea? Why do I see them? And I do not mean Franco's bird, nor the roasted chicken from *take away*, nor the conservative symbol. It does not interest me here or there. I do not talk about it here or there. Clouds are a band of orange stars. Here and now you are the protaganist. Dear sparrow. My beloved is dead. Do not twist the words of Catullus. Do not tattoo ashes in your mouth. Dear sparrow, born in what form? And I am not referring to the poem, I am not referring to a philosophy nor an art; yes to a space and smoke from all the hours in which I waited, in which I read, that in Madriz is a desert. From all the times that I fled. In which I do not have you.

cumplir veinte años
(2009-2010)

En aquel tiempo yo tenía veinte años
y estaba loco.
ROBERTO BOLAÑO

being twenty
(2009-2010)

At that time I was twenty years old
and was crazy.
ROBERTO BOLAÑO

CUMPLEAÑOS

Hoy todo me recuerda
a la pureza de los catorce años:

las manos de un viejo en su destierro,
el canto de Hildegard von Bingen y sus glúteos azotados,
la camisa del pijama desabrochada a propósito
para que algún hombre (solo un hombre)
se adentrase en el abismo del ojal.

Hoy todo me recuerda cruelmente
a aquellos días:

el mar desabrochado
el puente óxido en la estación de tren
un horizonte presumido
las uñas de mi padre.

Hoy cumplo veinte años

*(deshazte,
pureza)*

y culpo de nostalgia.
A esta memoria enumerada.

BIRTHDAY

Today everything reminds me
of the purity of being fourteen years old:

the hands of an old man in his banishment,
the song of Hildegard von Bingen and his butt whippings,
the pajama shirt unbuttoned on purpose
for some man (only one man)
to penetrate the abyss of the buttonhole.

Today everything reminds me viciously
of those days:

the unbuttoned sea
the oxidized bridge in the train station
the vain horizon
the nails of my father.

Today, I am twenty years old

(*purity,*
vanish)

and I blame nostalgia.
To this enumerated memory.

SENOS

Tengo un pecho más grande que otro.

Por eso los hombres me acarician
el más
abultado.

Son listos.
Pienso.
Es el instinto animal.

Mi pecho
mi seno
mi teta morada de mordiscos
de frío
de imperfección.

Solo tú eres perfecto
solo él,
os digo,
corazón grasiento,
él prefiere el olor a mierda
que el olor a
lejía

él y el perfecto defecto
de su barbilla cálida

de su caricia cálida

de su estéril *te quiero*.

BREASTS

I have one breast bigger than the other.

So men caress the one that is
more
bulky.

They are smart.
I think.
It's an animal instinct.

My chest
my breast
my tit purple from bites
from the cold
from imperfection.

Only you are perfect
only him,
I say,
greasy heart,
he prefers the smell of shit
to the smell of
bleach

he and the perfect defect
of his warm chin

from his warm touch

from his sterile *I love you.*

AMOR

Porque el amor es estéril,
existe el sexo.

LOVE

Because love is sterile,
sex exists.

OREJAS DE MOSCA

También tengo orejas de mosca.

Aunque no sé cómo son las orejas de mosca.

Ni siquiera sé si las moscas tienen orejas.

Y el zumbido.

El temblor impaciente de mis manos
antes de encontrarte.

Porque escucho con oídos de abeja,
de insecto,
de bicho loco:
bichito aplastado.

Mi pecho es el de un animal inmenso.

Rujo de mentira.

No conozco a ese dios.

Vuelo y casi ladro.

Creo que soy joven.

FLY'S EARS

I also have fly's ears.

Although I do not know how fly's ears are.

I do not even know if flies have ears.

And the buzz.

The impatient trembling of my hands
before I found you.

Because I hear with bee's ears,
of insect,
of crazy animal:
crushed little animal.

My chest is the one of an immense animal.

I fake roar.

I don't know that god.

I fly and almost bark.

I think I am young.

LADY BIRD

Antes de ser mujer
fui pájaro
y fui niña.

Antes de las tardes de sexo.

De las mañanas de sexo.

Antes de los días adúlteros

y adolescentes

abierta a otros
que no eras tú.

Fui pájaro sin acné.
Fui gorrión y mirlo.
Odié gaviotas.

Apenas susurré.

Hoy el color de mis alas
es el de todas las mujeres.

Por mi pecho y mis caderas.

Porque he crecido y he mutado.

Porque yo fui niña,

fui niña:

LADY BIRD

Before being a woman
I was a bird
and I was a girl.

Before the evenings of sex.

The mornings of sex.

Before the adulterous

and adolescent days

open to others
that were not you.

I was a bird without acne.
I was a sparrow and blackbird.
I hated seagulls.

Hardly whispered.

Today, the color of my wings
is that of all women.

For my chest and my hips.

Because I have grown and mutated.

Because I was a girl,

I was a girl:

y olvidé que la sangre no era
granate
sino blanca.

Y olvidé entonces mi infancia.

Como todas las mujeres.

and forgot that the blood was not
garnet
but white.

And then I forgot my childhood.

As all women.

ÁCIDA

embarazada de mí
FATENA AL-GURRA

Porque me embarazaste
nazco de ti
desnuda
y ácida.

Sangra mi estigma.

Sangra porque el verbo *sangrar*
es sinónimo
de buena literatura.

Porque la buena literatura
salva
a los inútiles,

a los vagos como yo.

A los vagos como mi vientre,
incapaz
de engendrarse solo,

a sí mismo,

sin tu semen,

solo.

Porque lánguida
nazco de la nada.

ACID

pregnant of me
FATENA AL-GURRA

Because you impregnated me
I am born of you
naked
and acidic.

My stigma bleeds.

It bleeds because the verb to bleed
is synonomous
of good literature.

Because good literature
saved
the useless ones,

the lazy ones like me.

The lazy ones like my belly
unable
to breed alone

itself,

without your semen,

alone.

Because languid
I am born from nothing.

En medio de todo esto.

Desnuda.

Ácida.

In the midst of all this.

Naked.

Acidic.

POETA SUICIDA

Todo rasurado:
hasta la última pestaña
de esta pesadilla monótona.
Todo rasurado.
Todo falso.
Imitación punk de una poeta muerta.

Si Pizarnik resucitó,
¿lo harás tú,
suicida idiota,
que miras desde el reflejo?

Todo rasurado,

¿coño o corazón?

eso qué importa cuando ambos huelen a vida,
cuando ambos sangran y tiñen de amor.

Todo rasurado para sentir mejor el hielo.
Todo frío.
Todo muy frío y hermoso.
Todo vacío, por última vez.

SUICIDAL POET

All shaved:
up to the last eyelash
from this monotonous nightmare.
All shaved.
All false.
Punk imitation of a dead poet.

If Pizarnik was resurrected,
so will you
suicidal idiot,
who spies from the reflection?

All shaved,

Cunt or heart?

that what matters when both smell of life,
when both bleed and stain from love.

All shaved to better feel the ice.
All cold.
All very cold and beautiful.
All empty, for the last time.

EL BELLO MUNDO ME PRODUCE ASCO

That's basically how I spent my twenties:
jealous and feeling bad about my self.
DENISE DUHAMEL

Detestaría mi juventud si fuera solo una excusa.

Detestaría el mundo.

Siento por él un absurdo apego.

THE BEAUTIFUL WORLD GIVES ME DISGUST

That's basically how I spent my twenties:
jealous and feeling bad about my self.
DENISE DUHAMEL

I would hate my youth was only an excuse.

I would hate the world.

I feel for it an absurd attachment.

FELACIÓN

No empujes la cabeza.
No empujes hacia adentro.

¿Quieres asesinarme?

No sientes la arcada como yo la siento.

No sientes la arcada arañando el corazón.

No sientes el fin del mundo en la punta
de la campanilla.

Ni el grumo que ahoga.

Ni el grumo que escuece.

Ni este placer inmenso de tenerme atragantada.

FELLATIO

Do not push the head.
Do not push inwards.

Do you want to murder me?

You do not feel the retch that I am.

You do not feel the retch scratching the heart.

You do not feel the end of the world in the top
of the uvula.

Nor the lump that drowns.

Nor the lump that stings.

Nor this immense pleasure of having me choked.

CELOS

No sé como decirte que no pienso en otros hombres:

raparme al cero,

raparme la palabra,

raspar con silencio

otras manos que no quiero.

JEALOUSY

I don't know how to tell you that I don't think of other men:

shave off to zero,

shave the word,

scrape with silence

other hands that I don't want.

MDMA

El matrimonio es esa boca
que apesta a cariño
y a MDMA.

MDMA

Marriage is this mouth
that stinks like afffection
and MDMA.

ESTACIÓN *ATOCHA RENFE*

Leer en el tren.

Destino Atocha.

[Atocha Puerta de Madrid.
Atocha espacial.
Atocha Muerte.]

Mirar a través de la ventana.

Amar cada piedra de las vías.

Esas piedras pulidas. Esas piedras cuadradas.

De dónde vienen.

Quién las fabrica.

Piedras. Gravilla gorda.

Diamantes brutos disfrazados de vulgaridad.

ATOCHA RENFE STATION

To read on the train.

Destination Atocha.

[Atocha Madrid's Door.
Atocha space.
Atocha death.]

To look through the window.

To love every stone of the pathways.

Those polished stones. Those square stones.

Where do they come from.

Who makes them.

Stones. Fat gravel.

Uncut diamonds disguised as vulgarity.

HUELO MUERTE

Todas las poetisas están muertas, dijo.
ROBERTO BOLAÑO

Espejito, espejito.

¿Acaso

soy joven?

¿Acaso

huelo a muerte?

I SMELL DEATH

All the poets are dead, he said.
ROBERTO BOLAÑO

Little mirror, little mirror.

Perhaps

I am young?

Perhaps

I smell death?

MENSONGE

Pasé veinte años diciendo:
Yo.

Ahora no sé nada de poesía.

LIE

I spent twenty years saying:
I.

Now I know nothing about poetry.

la tumba del marinero
(2010-2011)

sailor's grave
(2010-2011)

HUMAN AFTER ALL

La muerte no puede ser experimentada ni por los vivos ni por los muertos pero sí por los enfermos. Ocurre lo mismo con la piel: cuando estoy nerviosa me la arranco de cuajo, alrededor de los dedos, hasta que sangra, pero aun así, después de tanto dolor no consigo quitármela entera. A los muertos se les arranca la piel (¿lo hace el fuego? ¿lo hacen los gusanos? ¿lo hace el tiempo? poco importa). El enfermo se pela sin dolor, se quema sin fuego, se come los gusanos. En esta misma casa hay un enfermo. Decir enfermedad es decir locura. Vivo con un enfermo que se araña los brazos, que rompe los muebles con las uñas, que me muerde el corazón con su tristeza. Está loco y enfermo, pero sólo a veces. Lo amo y lo cuido, pero sólo siempre y los fines de semana. El amor no puede ser experimentado si no estás loco, o enfermo, o muy vivo o muy muerto. Tu abuelo murió y le cosieron la boca para que no soltara pus, para que no soltara moscas, para que nadie viera su obscena cara de placer: que sólo los locos muertos gozan así... porque morir nos hace eternos, tan eternos como las olas que evaporadas son nubes y que líquidas son cáncer. Cánceres como plural de cáncer, o bien, tumor, como plural de abrazos. Alguien me enseñó a dibujar el viento y era algo parecido a esto. Una onda en mi sonrisa, pensé, o bien, *amor, te he pedido perdón demasiadas veces*, escribió Ferrater. El viento era esto. Nacer era esto. Morir sin morir y sin enfermedad era esto. Decirte la verdad: estoy aquí y te necesito. Decirte la verdad era esto. Observo mi propia mano en una instantánea analógica, trato de tocar mi propia mano con mi propia mano, decía, mi propia sombra con la mano y no estoy tocando nada. Pero te necesito. Tengo las uñas pintadas de rojo, o, más bien, despintadas de rojo. Mi amigo el ruso me dijo que yo no era una buena mujer. Remarcaba la erre de "eres" y de "mujer". Tu no "erres" una buena "mujerr" porque llevas las uñas mal pintadas. Mal pintadas y mal cortadas y me arranco

HUMAN AFTER ALL

Death cannot be experienced neither for the living nor the dead but for the sick. The same applies to the skin: when I'm nervous it's ripped around the fingers until it bleeds, but still, after so much pain I do not get it out whole. The skin is also ripped from the dead (is it ripped by the fire? by the worms? by the time? It's not important). The sick is ripped without hurt, burn without fire, eats worms. In this house there is a sick person. To speak of the sickness is to speak of a craziness. I live with a sick patient who scratches his arms, breaks the furniture with his nails, bites my heart with his sadness. He is crazy and sick, but only sometimes. I love him and take care of him, but only always and on the weekends. Love cannot be experienced if you are not crazy, or sick, or very alive or very dead. Your grandfather died and sewed his mouth shut to not release puss, not to release flies, for anyone to see his obscene face of pleasure: only fools and the dead enjoy it like that… because death makes us eternal, as eternal as the waves that evaporated into clouds, and that liquid is cancer. Cancers as plural of cancer, or tumor, as the plural of hugs. Someone taught me to draw the wind and it was something like this. A wave in my smile, I thought, or maybe, *love, I have apologized too many times*, wrote Ferrater. The wind was this. Being born was this. Dying without dying and without a disease was this. To tell you the truth: I am here and I need you. To tell you the truth was this. I watch my own hand in an analog instant, I try to play my own hand with my own hand, I said, my own shadow with hand and I'm not touching anything. But I need you. I have red nail polish, or rather, unpainted red. My Russian friend told me that I was not a good woman. Remarked the rolling R's of "you" and of "woman." You "aRRRe" not good "womannn" because you have badly painted nails. Bad painted and badly cut and I rip the surrounding skin, "Ferraterr." "Deathhh." "Womannn." I feel

la piel de alrededor, "Ferraterr". "Morrirr". "Mujerr". Me siento salvaje cuando me arranco la sangre. Siento al mundo salvaje cuando la sangre cae al suelo. Quiero que nazcan hijos de esas pequeñas gotas. Que nazcan bestias marinas. Seres mitológicos. Pájaros gigantescos de esas gotas. Que baje Zeus y me folle también. Que baje hasta aquí la boca de mi loco enfermo y me haga fértil también. La vida no puede ser experimentada ni por los vivos ni por los muertos. Mamá me leía la *Iliada* y otras historias "para que aprendiera escenas, cuentos y vocabulario" Quieres ser periodista, me dijo, para eso tienes que conocer muchas palabras. Pobre ingenua ella ¡muchas palabras! Pobre ingenua yo ¡periodista! Respondí a mamá y ella rió algo perpleja. "Que para hablar del mundo sólo necesito conocer la palabra muerte". Niña repelente. Muerte repelente. La niñez no puede ser experimentada ni por los vivos ni por los muertos porque los vivos no lo recuerdan y los muertos amanecen sin piel. La niñez sólo puede ser experimentada por los enfermos y los locos, decía. Como la vida y como la muerte y como el amor, tal vez. Así es el luto. Una larga soledad acompañada. La soledad del enamorado loco. Del pájaro carnívoro. De la cama que no chirría. Del niño que no sabe imaginar.

wild when I rip my blood. I feel the wild world when blood falls to the ground. I want my children born from such small drops. I want marine beasts born. Mythological beings. Gigantic birds from such drops. I want Zeus to come down and fuck me too. I want down here my crazy sick patient's mouth and to make me fertile as well. Life cannot be experienced neither for the living nor for the dead. Mom read me *The Iliad* and other stories "to learn scenes, stories and vocabulary." To want to be a journalist, she said, for that you have to know many words. Poor naïve she was, many words! Poor naïve I was. Journalist! I responded and she laughed somewhat perplexed. "For what talk of the world I only need to know the word death." Nerdy girl. Nerdy death. The childhood cannot be experienced neither for the living nor for the dead because the living do not remember and the dead dawn skinless. The childhood can only be experienced by the sick and crazy, I said. As life and death and as love, perhaps. Mourning is just like that. A long accompanied loneliness. The loneliness of the crazy in love. Of the carnivorous bird. Of the bed that doesn't squeak. Of a child that doesn't know how to imagine.

EL VELATORIO DE TU ABUELO

Para que mi madre viva le tienen que abrir la boca.

Al resto de los muertos se la sellan.

YOUR GRANDFATHER'S WAKE

For my mother to live they have to open her mouth.

To the rest of the dead they seal it.

SAILOR'S GRAVE

Pacté con mi madre un tatuaje en el cuello.
Las dos compartiríamos marca,
las dos,
el sello de la tinta que nos une.

Sin embargo ahora
una cicatriz en el lugar íntimo
separa nuestras nucas para siempre.

SAILOR'S GRAVE

I made a pact with my mother a tattoo on the neck.
Both of us share a mark,
both,
an ink stamp that unites us.

However now
a scar in an intimate place
separates our napes forever.

CICATRICES

Mi abuelo tiene una cicatriz en el estómago.
Mi abuela tiene una cicatriz en el pecho.
Mi madre tiene una cicatriz en la garganta.
Mi padre tiene una cicatriz en la rodilla.
Mi amante tiene una cicatriz en el costado.
Mi vida no tiene cicatrices. Sólo manchas,
sólo aceite y tiempo quemado.
Sólo un rasguño.

SCARS

My grandpa has a scar on the stomach.
My grandma has a scar on the chest.
My mom has a scar on the throat.
My dad has a scar on the knee.
My lover has a scar on the side.
My life does not have scars. Only spots,
only oil and burnt time.
Only a scratch.

ÚLTIMO

No me protegen de las paredes vacías. No me protegen las chinchetas en el suelo de alquiler, de una habitación de alquiler, de una vida cara de alquiler que mis pulmones no soportan. No trato de dar pena: procuro dar asco. No trato la belleza: procuro mi delirio. No trato la juventud: comprendo lo infantil de mis facciones. Mi desánimo. Mis ganas de llorar. Nunca me levantaría de esta cama. Comería aquí. Defecaría justo aquí. Haría el amor bajo el colchón. Así. Con estos ojos. Así. La mañana es perversa con su luz. Nadie protege mi diario desprotegido. Mi vida desprotegida, que, lo sé, a veces ni siquiera se parece a esta que prometo.

LAST

They do not protect me from the empty walls. Do not protect me from the thumbtacks in the rented floor, from the rented room, from the rented expensive life that my lungs do not bear. I am not trying to look pathetic: I try to disgust. Do not treat the beauty: I procure bring my delirium. Do not treat the youth: I understand the infant of my features. My discouragement. My desire to cry. I would never get up from this bed. I'd eat here. I'd defecate just here. I'd make love under the sheets. Like this. With these eyes. Like this. Morning is perverse with its light. No one protects my unprotected diary. My unprotected life, that, I know, at times is not even like this one that I promise.

CARTA A LA MADRE

Me contaron que saber retórica es como saber amar con la palabra exacta, amar a un dios o a un pezón incluso si lleva veinte años sin donar su leche seca. Mustia. Su leche de jazmín de otoño. Natural. Pero tú odias el jazmín. Pero tú odias tanto el olor a jazmín. Cómo te extraño. Persuasivas las palabras de esos ojos. Me contaron. Me convencieron. Que saber amar no es como saber amar. O sí. Quizá. Amar, pero más fuerte.

LETTER TO THE MOTHER

They told me that knowing rhetoric is like knowing how to love with the exact word, to love a god or a nipple even if it has been twenty years without giving its dry milk. Blight. Its milk of jasmine of fall. Natural. But you hate jasmine. Smells so bad. I miss you. Persuasive words from those eyes. I was told. I was convinced. That knowing how to love is not like knowing how to love. Or yes. Maybe. Love, but stronger.

LA MUJER SIN ROSTRO

then i woke up
your parents were dancing so hard
ELLEN KENNEDY

Qué cara poner.

Qué rostro dentro de tu rosto

y dentro de tu rostro y qué tabique

nasal.

Qué cara poner

delante de tus padres

recién colocada

recién muerta

recién la sangre y la sangre

y qué sangre

poner

si no son tus venas.

No.

No son tus venas lo que corto

son otras uñas

THE FACELESS WOMAN

then i woke up
your parents were dancing so hard
ELLEN KENNEDY

What face to put.

What face inside of your face

and inside of your face and what nasal

septum.

What face to put

in front of your parents

freshly high

freshly dead

freshly the blood and the blood

and what blood

to put

if not your veins.

No.

Is not your veins what I cut

are other nails

son otros gestos

es otra mujer *la que me habita.*

No.

Mis padres bailan, locos,

bailan y engullen sushi

engullen pavo

se engullen a ellos mismos

primero los dedos luego

las tripas

luego...

Y hablan de libros

y me miran a los ojos

y me miran el rostro

pero qué rostro poner

cómo mentir a papá

cómo mentir a una madre enferma.

No estoy embarazada.

No tomo drogas.

are other gestures

is another woman *who lives in me.*

No.

My parents dance, crazy

dance and gobble sushi

gobble turkey

gobble up themselves

first fingers then

the guts

then…

And speak of books

and they look at my eyes

and they look at my face

but what face to put

how to lie to dad

how to lie to a sick mom.

I am not pregnant.

I do not do drugs.

No me lavo.

No tengo sexo.

No enseño las palmas de las manos.

No las estiro hasta romperlas.

No.

Aquí no hay polvo blanco.

¿Quién llama?

¿A qué hora llegas?

¿Por qué la ausencia?

No cocaína.

No,

padre.

Aquí, donde el cielo aclara.

No tengo rostro.

I do not wash myself.

I do not have sex.

I do not show the palms of my hands.

I do not stretch them until broken.

No.

Here I do not have white powder.

Who's calling?

At what time do you arrive?

Why are you missing?

No cocaine.

No,

dad.

Here, where the sky is clear.

I do not have a face.

MAL

Ni siquiera sé si me imaginas.

¿Me imaginas? Dímelo.

Dímelo. ¿Me imaginas

desnuda

desabotonada

detestable

me imaginas?

¿Piensas en mí cada noche?

¿Piensas en mí

como yo pienso en la muerte

en el mar

en las lúbricas golondrinas

cada noche?

Existo, entonces,

luego tiemblo.

Existo, entonces,

luego odio.

BAD

I do not even know if you picture me.

Do you picture me? Tell me.

Tell me. Do you picture me

naked

unbuttoned

detestable

Do you picture me?

You think about me every night?

You think about me

as I think about death

in the sea

in the lubricious swallows

every night?

I exist, therefore,

then I tremble.

I exist, therefore,

then I hate.

Existo, entonces.

Todo puede hacerme daño.

I exist, therefore

anything can damage me.

YO SÉ QUÉ

la pureza que te preguntaba
MAITE DONO

La pureza es este párpado.

La pureza es esta mano vieja, que mancha si acaricia.

La pureza es mi sexo diminuto.

La pureza es una media luna.

La pureza es la lengua cortada de mi madre.

La pureza es este poema.

La pureza es el pensamiento impuro.

La pureza es el aliento en la mañana.

La pureza es un cepillo lleno de pelos.

La pureza es una bañera negra llena de leche negra llena de pelos.

La pureza es esta copa, este vino, esta carne.

La pureza es una hostia.

La pureza es mi reflejo.

La pureza es candidiasis.

La pureza es diabetes.

I KNOW WHAT

the purity that I was asking you
MAITE DONO

Purity is this eyelid.

Purity is an old hand, stained that pets.

Purity is my diminute sex.

Purity is a half moon.

Purity is the tongue cut from my mother.

Purity is this poem.

Purity is impure thoughts.

Purity is the breath in the morning.

Purity is a brush full of hair.

Purity is a black bathtub full of black milk full of hair.

Purity is this cup, this wine, this meat.

Purity is a wafer.

Purity is my reflection.

Purity is thrush.

Purity is diabetes.

La pureza es miedo, sucio miedo asomándose.

La pureza es medicina.

La pureza es tu polla.

La pureza es nuestra casa en invierno.

La pureza es un calefactor.

La pureza da asco.

La pureza da asco.

La pureza da asco como un pájaro

que anida en la campana

de una iglesia

en la campana

de una cocina

en la campana

de una garganta.

Yo sé qué es la pureza.

La pureza es este país fuerte.

La pureza es la raza.

La pureza es lo casto.

Purity is afraid, dirty fear looming.

Purity is medicine.

Purity is your cock.

Purity is our house in winter.

Purity is a heater.

Purity is disgusting.

Purity is disgusting.

Purity is disgusting as a bird

that nests in the bell

of a church

in the fan

of a kitchen

in the uvula

of a throat.

I know what purity is.

Purity is this strong country.

Purity is the race.

Purity is the chaste.

La pureza es el himen.

La pureza es el pájaro y el himen.

La pureza da asco

es tierna

es cerda

es única.

Yo sé qué es la pureza.

Yo sé qué es.

Purity is the hymen.

Purity is the bird and the hymen.

Purity is disgusting

is tender

is dirty

is unique.

I know what purity is.

I know what it is.

EN CAMA

A veces no quiero que llegue el día

siguiente.

Para qué.

Para sufrir el sol.

Y condenar las horas.

Condenada a las horas.

Y condenar los segundos.

No quiero que llegue.

Quedémonos aquí.

Muy quietos.

IN BED

Sometimes I do not want the following day

to arrive.

For what.

To suffer the sun.

And condemn the hours.

Condemned to the hours.

And condemn the seconds.

I do not want it to arrive.

Let's stay here.

Very still.

COMA DIABÉTICO

Tú me diste una boca.

Mi madre me dio este páncreas.

La Ciencia me dio insulina.

Dios no me dio nada salvo miedo en un puñado de azúcar.

DIABETIC COMA

You gave me a mouth.

My mother gave me this pancreas.

Science gave me insulin.

God did not give me anything except fear in a handful of sugar.

The bird is flying above the forest. One wing is bent. He is trying to make sense of the hole in his chest.

Dorothea Laskey

Algunas aclaraciones del traductor y la autora

"El cri-cri de las margaritas" es un verso de Federico García Lorca en Poeta en Nueva York.

"Sick rose" es un homenaje a ese mismo verso de William Blake.

"El neón de siempre" es el título de un relato de David Foster Wallace.

"Cave lunam" es una versión del famoso "cave canem" en latín.

Se introduce por primera vez "Madriz", una forma particular de referirse a Madrid. "Avenida de América" es la estación de autobuses del Norte de la ciudad.

Alejandra Pizarnik es una conocida poeta en el mundo hispano que se suicidó joven

"El bello mundo me produce asco" es un homenaje a la poeta española Carmen Jodra

"Atocha" es la estación de trenes más conocida de España

"Human after all" es una canción de Daft Punk

"Lo sé qué" es un homenaje a la poeta española Maite Dono y a sus versos: *Qué es la pureza? Tú lo sabes? Jódeme.*

Some clarifications from the author and translator

"The cricket call of daisies" is a verse from Federico García Lorca in the book *Poet in New York*.

"Sick rose" is a tribute to the same verse from William Blake.

"Good old Neon" is the title of a story from David Foster Wallace.

"Cave lunam" is a version of the famous "cave canem" in Latin.

Introduced for the first time is "Madriz", a particular form of referring to Madrid. "Avenida de América" is the bus station in the north of the city.

Alejandra Pizarnik is a well-known poet in the Hispanic world that committed suicide at a young age.

"The Beautiful world gives me disgust" is a tribute to the Spanish poet Carmen Jodra

"Atocha" is the most well-known train station in Spain.

"Human after all" is a song by Daft Punk.

"I know what" is a tribute to the Spanish poet Maite Dono and her verses: *What is purity? Do you know? Fuck me.*

Nota de la autora

Los poemas aquí presentes, como ya señalamos al comienzo de la edición, pertenecen a distintas obras que he escrito o publicado a lo largo de mis primeros veinte años de vida. Se trata de una pequeña muestra de esos libros que en total (Estar enfermo, Poetry is not dead, Pensamientos estériles y Sailor's Grave) sumarían unas 300 páginas de poemas, citas, y textos en prosa. Hubiera resultado imposible resumir todos esos momentos en apenas diez o doce poemas de cada libro, pero creo que la selección que aquí os presentamos es fiel a lo que desde hace ya casi seis años vengo intentando plasmar en el papel.

Bluebird and Other Tattoos marca además una etapa muy clara de mi vida, y es aquella en la que empecé a leer literatura joven extranjera, de todas partes del mundo, pero sobre todo norteamericana. Leer a Tao Lin, a Dorothea Lasky, a Kendra Grant Malone o a Richard Chiem, entre otros tantos, me ha dado la oportunidad de hacer muchísimos proyectos, traducciones, antologías de poesía y difusión cultural. En un mundo en el que parece que la literatura importa poco, la comunicación en Facebook, Twitter o Tumblr con esos autores y la creación de redes entre todos es un paso muy fuerte hacia algo mejor.

Fue en septiembre de 2010 cuando decidí comprar *Everything is Quiet* de Kendra Grant Malone gracias a una recomendación que había visto en HTML Giant. Me sorprendió y me hizo mucha ilusión que después de pedirlo en la web de Scrambler Books su editor Jeremy Spencer me escribiera para agradecer la compra. Parece ser que, además, Jeremy había visto una entrevista que pocos días antes me habían hecho para 3AM Magazine y entonces nos pusimos a hablar de literatura e intercambiamos libros. Un día, después de mandarle mi recién salido del horno Poetry is not dead, me propuso publicar algo con él y ese se convirtió en uno de los mejores momentos de mi vida literaria. Publicar es emocionante y que te traduzcan lo es más. Ver tu vida escrita en otro idioma es tan extraño como maravilloso.

Author's Note

The poems presented here, as we mentioned at the beginning of the edition, belong to different works that have been written or published over the first twenty years of my life. This is a small sample of those books that in total (Estar enfermo, Poetry is not dead, Pensamientos estériles y La tumba del mariner) would add up to about 300 pages of poems, quotes and prose. It would have been impossible to summarize all of those moments in just ten or twelve poems from each book, but I think that the selection that we present here is true to what for almost six years I have been trying to capture on paper.

Bluebird and Other Tattoos also marks a stage that is very clear in my life, and it is one in which I began to read foreign literature by young writers, from all over the world, but mostly American. Reading Tao Lin, Dorothea Laskey, Kendra Grant Malone and Richard Chiem, among many others has given me the opportunity to do many projects, translations, poetry anthologies and cultural diffusion. In a world where it seems that literature is of little importance, communication on Facebook, Twitter or Tumblr with these authors and networking among all is a very strong step toward something better.

It was in September 2010 when I decided to buy *Everything is Quiet* by Kendra Grant Malone thanks to a recommendation I had seen on HTML Giant. I was surprised and excited that after ordering it from the site Scrambler Books, the editor Jeremy Spencer wrote me to thank me for my purchase. It appears that in addition, Jeremy had seen an interview a few days before that I had done for 3AM magazine and then we proceeded to talk about literature and exchanged books. One day, after sending my freshly baked book *Poetry is not dead,* he proposed to publish something with it and that became one of the highlights of my literary life. Publishing is emotional and will translate into something more. To see your life written in another language is as strange as it is wonderful.

Por esos motivos este Bluebird and Other Tattoos está dedicado principalmente a Jeremy Spencer, por la confianza y el amor que ha depositado, desde tan tan tan lejos, en mis textos. Ojalá este libro sea un motivo para conocernos en persona, no muy tarde.

También quería agradecer el apoyo y el coleg ueo a Jake Fournier, Tao Lin, Megan Boyle, Alec Niedenthal, Richard Chiem, Stephen Tully Dierks, Cassandra Troyan, Ana C., Noah Cicero, Ani Smith, Dorothea Lasky, Ellen Kennedy, Kendra Grant Malone, Kat Dixon, Ken Baumman, Gabby Gabby, Jacob Steinberg... y muchos, muchos más... leerles y compartir cosas con ellos todos los días es siempre genial. Por supuesto sin mis editores, mis amigos y mis lectores españoles esto no hubiera sido posible. Gracias a ellos, y a Betty Blue, que pone los pájaros en este cielo. Y no podría dejar de pronunciar y escribir todas las sílabas de Ibrahím Berlín (aka Antonio J. Rodríguez), mi chico. Él está en todos los poemas y para él son.

Es viernes, 19 de agosto de 2011. A día de hoy tengo cinco tatuajes en mi cuerpo: una luna en la muñeca, un dibujo de Betty Blue en el brazo, la palabra infinite en el pecho, un ancla -Sailor's Grave- en el antebrazo y un único tatuaje en color: un pájaro azul, exactamente una golondrina, justo encima del corazón, rodeado por unos versos del poema *Bluebird* de Charles Bukowski. Sé que me tatuaré más y sé que escribiré más. De momento esto es todo.

Desde Madrid/Barcelona.

Luna.

For these reasons this *Bluebird and Other Tattoos* is mainly dedicated to Jeremy Spencer, for the trust and love that has been deposited from so so so far, in my writing. Hopefully this book will be a reason to meet in person, sooner rather than later.

I also wanted to acknowledge the support and the camaraderie of Jake Fournier, Tao Lin, Megan Boyle, Alec Niedenthal, Richard Chiem, Stephen Tully Dierks, Cassandra Troyan, Ana C., Noah Cicero, Ani Smith, Dorothea Lasky, Ellen Kennedy, Kendra Grant Malone, Kat Dixon, Ken Baumman, Gabby Gabby, Jacob Steinberg...and many many more...to read and share things with them every day is always great. Of course, without my editors, my friends and my Spanish readers none of this would have been possible. Thanks to them, and to Betty Blue for putting birds in this sky. And I could not leave without pronouncing and writing all of the syllables of Ibrahím Berlín (aka Antonio J. Rodríguez), my boy. He is in all of the poems and they are all for him.

It's Friday, August 19, 2011. Today I have five tattoos on my body: a moon on the wrist, a picture from Betty Blue on the arm, the word infinite on the chest, an anchor- Sailor's Grave- on the forearm and a single tattoo in color: a bluebird, exactly a swallow, just above the heart, surrounded by a few lines of the poem *Bluebird* by Charles Bukowski. I know that I will tattoo more and write more. For now, this is all.

From Madrid/Barcelona.

Luna

Luna Miguel was born on November 6, 1990 in Madrid, but lives in Barcelona, where she works as a journalist, translator and editor.

She has authored the following poetry books *Estar enfermo* (La Bella Varsovia, 2010), *Poetry is not dead* (DVD, 2010), *Pensamientos estériles* (Cangrejo Pistolero, 2011) and *La tumba del marinero* (forthcoming, April 2013) as well as the story *Exhumación* (Alpha Decay, 2010), written together with her husband, Antonio J. Rodríguez.

Excerpts of her work have been translated into English, French, Italian, Portuguese, Dutch and Russian with two of her books having been published outside of Spain: *Bluebird and Other Tattoos* (Scrambler Books, 2012) in the USA, and *Musa ammalata* (Damocle Edizioni, 2012) in Italy.

She has kept a blog since the age of 15 which can be found at: www.lunamiguel.com

www.scramblerbooks.com